To Forgive God!

To Forgive God!

DR PETER GASIOROWSKI

Copyright © 2016 Dr Peter Gasiorowski.

All rights reserved. No part of this book may be used or reproduced by any means, graphic, electronic, or mechanical, including photocopying, recording, taping or by any information storage retrieval system without the written permission of the author except in the case of brief quotations embodied in critical articles and reviews.

WestBow Press books may be ordered through booksellers or by contacting:

WestBow Press
A Division of Thomas Nelson & Zondervan
1663 Liberty Drive
Bloomington, IN 47403
www.westbowpress.com
1 (866) 928-1240

Because of the dynamic nature of the Internet, any web addresses or links contained in this book may have changed since publication and may no longer be valid. The views expressed in this work are solely those of the author and do not necessarily reflect the views of the publisher, and the publisher hereby disclaims any responsibility for them.

Any people depicted in stock imagery provided by Thinkstock are models, and such images are being used for illustrative purposes only.
Certain stock imagery © Thinkstock.

Scripture quotations taken from the New American Standard Bible®, Copyright © 1960, 1962, 1963, 1968, 1971, 1972, 1973, 1975, 1977, 1995 by The Lockman Foundation. Used by permission. (www.Lockman.org)

This book is a work of non-fiction. Unless otherwise noted, the author and the publisher make no explicit guarantees as to the accuracy of the information contained in this book and in some cases, names of people and places have been altered to protect their privacy.

ISBN: 978-1-5127-4059-2 (sc)
ISBN: 978-1-5127-4058-5 (e)

Library of Congress Control Number: 2016942639

Print information available on the last page.

WestBow Press rev. date: 05/25/2016

Thank You!

Without my children, this book would never have existed. They wrote the most difficult part with me. But without Laura and John Keefer, I would never have gone through the process of forgiveness. Without Pam and Steve Moga, I would never have written a word. Without Susan and Bruce, I would never smile again. I also want to express very special gratitude to Wheatland Salem United Methodist Church in Naperville for what they did in the lives of my family.

Contents

Foreword ix

CHAPTER 1 The Accident...1

CHAPTER 2 The Runaway... 11

CHAPTER 3 Life and Shadow in Neverland................43

CHAPTER 4 Forgiveness 101 51

Epilogue 59

Foreword

I remember the phone call vividly.

To this day every time the calendar flips another page into December, my thoughts go to my friend Piotr. Since 2003 we have stayed in touch on the anniversary of his wife's death.

Both of us were national leaders, developing leaders with the Arrow Leadership Program. Piotr in Poland, Carson in Canada. We love the Lord and serve him, and to have an accident like this take place made no sense. What a loss!

When Piotr asked if I would read his manuscript and write a foreword, I was interested to read it myself. It was good, I thought, that Piotr was putting his thoughts and experience down in writing—words that you now hold and are published so they can be of assistance to many others.

We live in a world where not very many people are truly authentic. So many around us, ourselves included, try to hide what's really going on inside of us. This can be especially true for those in ministry or professional life. I have worked with leaders for almost two decades and in that time have met so many who have very few friends. I mean the kind of friends you can be real with. As you read this book, you are hearing from a man who is being authentic—honest, open, and candid—but in doing so he helps us pull back the curtain in our own lives and our need to forgive.

Imagine being in Piotr's situation. You'll wince as you read about his being suddenly thrust into trauma. Hurting, exhausted, and overwhelmed, he is left alone with the challenge of raising two children. With the intense grief, it doesn't surprise me at all to read of the struggle to forgive God. The one whom you would take refuge, protection, and safety in is the one you are talking to right now. Gosh, we have a difficult time forgiving other people. Imagine the need to come to a place where you realize you must forgive God. How do you have that conversation? This book will help.

Forgiveness can often seem impossible, but it is a critical element to our healing over any hurt in our lives. If we refuse to forgive, it will actually block our healing and begin to make us into people we do not want to be. We cannot ignore it.

Do you have someone you need to forgive right now? Are you withholding forgiveness to God about something that is happening your life or in the life of another one you love? Most people have someone they can blame for something. I commend these words to you from one who was hurt deeply and shares his journey of avoidance, running away, disorientation, helplessness, and then his return to God's way of dealing with it. What is God's way? Forgiving.

Years ago I heard a speaker say that forgiveness is setting the prisoner free from bondage, only to discover that the prisoner was you!

Peter's book came to me at God's perfect time. You see, we share something else in common now. My wife, Brenda, died August 11, 2015. I now understand from my circumstance the journey that my brother has been on. You will find as you read this that forgiveness is about getting your heart right with God. Ultimately, it's all about your relationship with God. I know you will grow through reading *To Forgive God* as Peter shares with openness his circular journey in understanding forgiveness.

Rev. Dr. Carson N Pue
Author of *Mentoring Leaders: Wisdom for Developing Character, Calling and Competency*
www.carsonpue.net

Chapter 1

The Accident

"Zibi, I am sorry. We had a fender bender, but they are finishing examining us, and we should soon be on our way! I think I can see our car at the parking lot. We will be a little late, but we are going to make it!"

I have never managed to figure out how he was able to keep a cool head in that situation. He had spoken to the nurse before and learned the truth. He did not reveal it to me. It was only a few hours later that I realized that Friday would forever change the life of our family.

It was December 2003. Anne and I were very excited about this trip to the Masuria Lake District to visit my friend Zibi. Two weeks earlier, I came back from a trip abroad, and important documents were awaiting my signature.

It was supposed to be a new beginning in my professional career. A few months earlier, I stepped down as a pastor in a place Anne and I had served for sixteen years. We believed the forthcoming months would be much more fortunate for our family.

The kids were happy that we would go away to Zibi's for a couple of days, leaving them alone at home. They excitedly encouraged their mom to go with me.

It was Friday, December 5. Anne and I woke up early and had coffee before heading out. It was still dark outside when we set off.

The weather felt more like autumn than winter. Rain was drizzling; it was quite warm but still somewhat unpleasant. I knew the road by heart. I had covered this distance many times each month on my way to church council meetings and lectures at the seminary.

The kids woke up a little later. Joanne, a junior high student, urged Lucas to take a shower, get dressed, and eat his breakfast. At that time, he still listened to her without a hint of objection. It all went smoothly enough for them to make it to school on time.

Lucas will never forget that Friday.

Christmastime was near, and each class was supposed to decorate their classroom. We were competing to see who could make the longest ornament chain. Polish lessons had just started when the principal came in. He said somebody had come to pick me up and that I was dismissed. I merrily went on to grab my jacket. It turned out that my mother's friend had come to pick me up. She did not explain anything.

"You'll know everything once we get back home," she said.

Already waiting at home were my sister, my aunt (Mom's sister), and her friend, who was a doctor. She gave me a pill. She said it was for the flu, but now I know it was a nerve pill. Fifteen minutes later, Joanne took me to our room and put me on the bed.

She sat in front of me, held my hand, and said, "Mom and Dad had an accident. Dad is okay, but Mom is dead."

On Friday, December 5, Joanne started with physics, which was one of her least-favorite subjects. The teacher was about to summon somebody to the blackboard when another teacher entered the classroom.

She told me to follow her to the principal's office. On our way, she held my hand with a strangely firm grip. We almost sprinted down the stairs. I saw some people from our church in the office. *Why are they here?* I thought. The principal said that my parents had been in an accident and that Dad was all right. He then added that Mom was dead! The long silence that swept in haunted me for a long time afterward. I wanted to call Dad, but they wouldn't let me, as he didn't know anything yet. I called Uncle Zibi. After all, my parents were going to visit him.

My friend's mom arrived shortly after, and we went home. Mrs. Helen, Mom's friend, was a doctor. She gave anxiety medication to Lucas. Afterward, I took him to his room and told him about Mom's death. Lucas started to choke. Mrs. Helen stepped in and told him to breathe.

He cried so much! He took our family picture, and we both cried as we lay in the bed together. Lucas fell asleep. Somebody went to pick up Dad, but I didn't know when they would come back.

Many hours passed. Our friends took Lucas in for the night, and I stayed home, waiting for Dad to arrive.

When he came in, he looked as if he had escaped from a hospital, with bloodstains on his clothes and a badly bruised face. When Lucas came back, we sat in the room together for a long time. Dad said he didn't know what was going to happen next.

"But we are going to be all right!" he added.

October 2004. I am staring at the place that still bears marks of what happened ten months ago. I still can't remember anything.

A man approaches me.

"Are you looking for someone? I know everyone in town, so I might be able to help."

"I'm looking for my wife," I answer.

The man looks at me closely.

"Oh, it was you who fell on your knees and begged me to help you get your wife out of the car 'cause you couldn't do it yourself."

In a flashback, I see our demolished car and Anne still in her seat. I can't undo the seatbelt, and she is not helping me!

Another flashback. I am sitting next to Annie in the ambulance, contorting with nausea. At around six thirty in the morning, we are in hospital. I am begging the doctors to save my wife. I remember a nurse saying they would take Annie for a check-up. She gives me an injection and lays me in a bed. It is she who phones Zibi, as his number is the only one I can recall. She tells him the truth before handing me the phone.

We only exchange a few words before I fall asleep.

I do not know how long I was asleep. When I wake up, I go to look for Annie. I peek inside several rooms until somebody rushes me out. I bump into the nurse who called Zibi.

"Where is she?" I ask.

I see tears in the nurse's eyes. She doesn't have to say anything else.

I think I have to return home as soon as possible.

To Joanne and Lucas.

Life before the Accident

Born in 1965, I grew up in a typical family. I had no major problems at school; I read every book I came across. I attended religion lessons at a class by our church. I was fourteen when I read the Bible. I noticed certain discrepancies between what the Bible and the catechism said.

I asked our religion teacher about the differences on several occasions. The priest was very nice. He played football with us and organized club meetings, but he failed to take my doubts seriously.

"You are too young to read the Bible," he said when I asked to speak with him once again.

Something snapped inside me at that moment. I was in eighth grade, and I stopped going to church. I started skipping religion lessons.[1] My mother asked me to at least wait until my confirmation. I listened to her and accepted the sacrament.

More than twenty years later I was … a pastor. I had a wife, Anne, and two children, Joanne and her four-year-younger brother, Lucas. However, before it came to that, my life, including the spiritual one, used to twist and turn in many directions.

At the turn of the 1980s, my visits in church were

---

[1] Many years later, I graduated in fundamental theology at the Pontifical Academy of Theology in Cracow, which helped me better understand the Catholic theology and look at my previous doubts from a broader perspective.

TO FORGIVE GOD!

seldom at best. Nobody at home expected that of me anymore.

I became a hippie. I still attended school, but I spent the afternoons with other hippies. I did drugs.

After about two years of that lifestyle, I met a girl. I liked her a lot, so I went with her to a summer camp—which turned out to be a Christian one.

I don't know why, but I started seeking a new relationship with God. It took me two years to fully convert. I ceased to be a hippie, and I gave up drugs. My friend passed away from a drug overdose at that time. We used to get high together. It occurred to me that God had thrown me a lifeline. Repentance saved both my soul and my earthly life.

I was twenty years old when I first met Anne. She was a year younger than I was and she accepted Christ as her savior at the beginning of our relationship. We got married three years later. Anne's mom literally dropped a hot iron on the floor when she learned her future son-in-law was studying at a theological college.

We started a family and had our ups and downs. One of the newspapers even published an interview with us about our family lifestyle. A pastor's family made a good topic for the media. How many wives can say that their husband is a priest? How many children in Poland have a father who wears a clerical collar?[2]

I served in my first congregation for two years. I was dreaming of moving to the Masuria Lake District—clean water, pristine woods, and fresh air! I thought it was the best thing that could happen to our family. Anne did not share my enthusiasm, however, as she preferred living in the city.

One day we were visited by my direct superior, who asked if we wanted to move to Cracow. I hesitated, but Annie eagerly agreed. We moved a month before our daughter came into the world. Four years later, our son was born. And so we stayed, living in the big city for the next sixteen years. Having taken on new duties, I became more and more engaged in my ministry, meetings, conferences, and trips abroad, which we would take together as the years went by, and frequent visits from many guests in our tiny apartment.

Suddenly, the tide turned against us. Annie became pregnant; we called it a nice, twin surprise. However, in the sixth month, one of the babies turned out to be dead, and the other was poisoned, with no chance of survival. The doctors miraculously managed to save Annie.

It took us some time before we finally came to terms with that loss.

Unfortunately, bad fortune continued to haunt us. I

---

[2] In Poland, Catholicism is by far the most numerous denomination, creating a stereotypical image of the priest living in celibacy.

fell ill with hepatitis C, and doctors gave me only a few years to live. I underwent painful treatment that lasted a whole year. I received over two hundred injections, and every other day I had to withstand insufferable muscle pains. Doctors were amazed at my recovery, except for the fact that a cancerous lump developed in my thyroid as a result of the treatment. As soon as they saw I was fit, the doctors removed my whole thyroid. Even today, I still need to take special medication.

In spite of our health problems, we kept on working. I was a pastor, and Annie set up an English language school together with her friends. We managed to reconcile our family life with work and ministry. We expressed our love for God through our service. We were a normal pastoral family devoted to the church.

Sixteen years with Annie was a time of joy and successes but also hardships, failures, and doubts. This is how life goes …

My was world shattered on December 5, 2003.

Unemployed at that time, I was left alone with two kids. I was haunted nonstop by the fear of them being taken away. I was also afraid I would be found guilty of causing the accident. Because, I am still unable to clearly recall what has happened, after more than ten years.

The court sentence was in my favor. According to the judge, the accident was caused by the driver who lost control over his overloaded truck.

I was surrounded by many wonderful people after the

accident. Members of my former congregation, colleagues from different churches, people I barely knew—they all took care of me and my children.

But there were also those who would ask me what I had done in order to deserve such punishment from God. Others believed me to be like the biblical Job, whose faith was being put to the test. I knew that they only said that to console me and give me strength, but such comparisons were driving me mad. After all, Job had also lost his children!

Then, twenty-two years after my conversion and sixteen years after my marriage, I started praying the only prayer I could bear in my heart: "God, please leave me and my family alone!"

I was convinced that after hurting me so much, after failing to hear my pleas for the miracle of resurrection, He could not wish for my forgiveness! I waged a war against God that would last for a few years. Each day, as I believed at that time, would bring me new reasons to challenge Him.

"No, I shall never forgive You this," I decided.

Chapter 2

The Runaway

If we fail to forgive, we allow the hurt and tragic experiences to build an altar in our hearts in front of which we can't help but fall to our knees. Even subconsciously, we try to remember how much we have suffered. We find plenty of reasons not to forgive, and we read any sign of doubt from others as a lack of understanding and sensitivity.

The sense of injustice and pain leads us to develop a peculiar type of pride. We believe nobody knows what we feel inside and nobody will ever understand. Only we know, and good luck to those who would even try to walk in our shoes!

The wound breeds arrogance that places us above everything and everyone who cannot properly relate to our suffering.

The simplest things and activities, which had to that point never taken great effort, would evoke anger and a feeling of rejection in me. It hit me the most while I was trying to cook. I had never done it before. I used to help Annie sometimes, but I couldn't do it on my own.

It happened soon after the accident. I was making dinner. It wasn't going very well, so I called my sister and asked how to flavor soup. I heard, "A pinch of salt, but not too much."

Okay, but how much is a *pinch* of salt? Is it as much as a teaspoon? Do you hold the salt in two or three fingers? How should I know when it's too much?

It makes me laugh today, but at that time I sat down and started to cry.

A few years later, my daughter asked me what color to pick for her prom dress. Color? What difference does it make?

I had been hurt and my whole world turned upside down. Nothing would ever be the same. It was painful to discover that the sun would still go up every day, that life would drag on tediously like a heavy train down the infinite rails, except there was no station to hop off board.

There are those who do hop off, forcing the train called life to stop. However, I was convinced from the very beginning that such an option would bring no solution to my problem.

Suffering only consolidates our convictions. Filled with grief, unable to forgive, we become runaways.

The escape can take various forms. Some try to repress whatever happened, and some even deny that anything took place. Nevertheless, every time somebody fails to forgive, he or she embarks on a journey—a journey with no destination that allows us not to deal with things that hurt. A chance to numb the pain.

It seems that by running away, one calls for justice in this unjust world.

And so I started to run; it was my great escape. I ran not to reach the finish line. I ran because it helped me to forget.

It sounds so paradoxical: when we are hurt, we do not want to remember the cause, but on the other hand, it is the very memory of hurt that becomes the focus of our attention.

Hurt, wounded, deceived, we demand compensation. We wait for a full redress of our loss. When robbed, we hope for the stolen goods to return to us. When deceived, we expect the truth to be a valid remedy. When used, we wish to receive something in return; there has to be justice, after all! It is not always likely, but we still anticipate it.

Paradoxically, at the same time, somewhere within the vast space of our thoughts lurks a feeling that our loss is enormous, too big to ever be fully redressed. This suspicion also reinforces our determination. We cannot forgive! We believe it to be the only right decision.

Disillusioned, filled with pain, we start to demand compensation more and more intensely. We do not forgive because we are waiting for the culprit to apologize, for the villain to be punished, for the rat to admit his guilt. We deem it necessary due to the extent of our loss and pain. And so we wait, failing to face the reality, fixed on our conviction that we have every right to be hurt.

But the pain keeps growing … It does not occur to us that it is this lack of forgiveness that strengthens the pain. We do not accept the fact that the will of the other party is irrelevant in the act of forgiving, as it only comes as an internal motion of the victim to give up on his claims. Forgiveness requires us to touch the wound, carefully examine every injury, every loss. It is ever so painful.

This is why the majority of those who don't forgive decide to run away. I ran because I wanted to run away from everything that my life was; I wanted to run from everything that connected me with Him.

He deceived me and caused harm to me and my children, after all!

And then he fell silent.

"It must be part of the plan," I heard as words of consolation.

"What kind of plan is this if it hurts so much?" I rebelled. "The God I believed in was a good God, who had nothing to do with evil, who would not let my foot strike against a stone. It was Him who was to make me lie down in green pastures."

Every word that hinted at the existence of some plan in which me and my feelings did not matter only reaffirmed

TO FORGIVE GOD!

my decision—*I will never forgive*! I would not listen to people arguing that I had to forswear my emotions for the sake of some divine plan.

"Are we but mere pawns, driven by a mysterious, whimsical God, who does not care what we feel?" I wondered in sorrow.

I am very well aware that one should not always succumb to one's emotions, but like every victim before me, I had many arguments to defend my decision. I asked, "Why deny that which *is*? If the Bible tells the truth about God and if He really wants to wipe my tears, then why is He ignoring my tears just now?"

God is a thoughtful and caring father. Not always does He agree with our feelings, sometimes teaching us how to let them go but definitely not ignoring them. Defiance is a stance that strikes against the dignity and value of other human beings. When we are ignored, we feel disrespected! An oppressor is somebody who does not respect us or our dignity. God made us the pinnacle of His creation, offering us love and respect. I believe that God respects me. Therefore, to Him, I am an individual being, not a means to an end. He, by limiting Himself, gave me a right to freedom, to my own opinion and choices.

I have been made in the image of God (*imago Dei*), and I have been privileged to freedom and constant development—transformation (Greek: *metanoia*). I believe that dignity (*dignitas hominis*) and respect relate to every human being. Everybody has a right to dignity and respect, regardless of their roots or social status. Acclaim, however, is something to be earned. It has to be obtained through one's own effort. Too often we fail to see the difference between respect and acclaim. It is also too easy for us to forget respect for other people because of their feelings and thoughts. All the same, every human deserves respect as God's creation. By failing to respect other people, we deprive ourselves of dignity. One will never earn acclaim this way.

Passed by the European Council, the Charter of Fundamental Rights states in its first article, "Human dignity is inviolable. It must be respected and protected." The Christian idea of dignity is rooted in the concept of the transcendent God and the naturalistic—in the very fact of human existence. They both boil down to one thing: every man deserves respect.

Through forgiveness, God restores dignity and expresses respect for His own creation. Not only has sin detached us from the Maker, but it also deprived us of dignity that lies at the basis of a harmonious coexistence with Him. Therefore, God deals with human guilt, but also restores our dignity, by forgiving.

The worst thing is that when we are running, we do not notice how we strip ourselves of dignity ascribed to us by God. We do not realize that by defying Him, we rob ourselves of respect that is a privilege of everybody, regardless of their roots, social status, skin color, experiences, and struggles. The loss of dignity accompanies the runaway at every point of their escape. They become extremely sensitive and feel like after a break-in, as if somebody violated their home and went through their stuff, touching the clothes, pictures, and belongings.

We are dealing with what psychology calls the posttraumatic stress disorder (PTSD). This state hinders normal functioning and occurs in the aftermath of a tragic event. It may be a result of war, torture, shooting, rape, natural disaster, burglary, terrorist attack, assault, kidnapping, captivity, humiliation or bullying at school, submission into foster care, violence, reenactment of trauma, sexual harassment, domestic violence, melee fight, mobbing, human trafficking, medical error, child abuse, accident, mugging, human rights violation, slavery, poverty, submission, disease, disability, mutilation, loss of loved ones, or any other sudden and traumatic event.

It can be also caused by a sudden threat to life of oneself and one's relatives, or even an indirect participation in such an event (e.g., witnessing a plane crash).

It is a natural response of the human psyche to situations beyond the limits of its resistance. It's a mental wound that is not a disease, per se, and had not existed before the traumatic experience. It causes the suffering to be reexperienced over and over again. Ordinary events can constantly evoke the trauma and summon images one would rather forget. Such flashbacks can cause us to lose touch with reality (e.g., relive an accident for a few seconds, hours, or even days).

The flashbacks can occur in the shape of images, sounds, smells, or feelings, causing the person suffering from PTSD to believe everything to be happening again.

In unforgiveness, we also keep living through our grievance and hurt. We reminisce over our experiences, reliving them and allowing them to take control. We do not see ourselves as deserving dignity and respect. We also strive not to view the guilty person or humankind in general in such categories. It is not about one's merits, suggesting acclaim, but about the God-given dignity. This is why all forms of defiance against this dignity also go against the nature of God.

But it does not occur to the harmed. They feel deprived of dignity!

The question is: if I was not respected, would my love for God have any value? He is not interested in love born out of necessity, emotional manipulation, or hopelessness.

God does not wish us to need Him (even though we do); God wishes us to want Him. The Maker wishes us to live with him as a consequence of free will, to which He empowered us Himself. Therefore, when we do not feel respected, we have another reason not to forgive. The bad experience itself affects our sense of value, and remaining in unforgiveness, reminiscing over grievance, failing to reject the pain not only causes us to overlook our own value but also blocks us from observing it all around us. After all, everything about the sufferers screams that nothing and nobody makes sense!

TO FORGIVE GOD!

In order to forgive, I have to observe the dignity of those I am forgiving.

It is through forgiveness that I regain my dignity and value. I also give back one's freedom, which is fundamental to dignity, and cease to hold both myself and the culprit captive to the past. I seclude the person from the evil that transpired. By forgiving, I do not allow grievance to govern our relationship. Forgiveness is a gift to the other person. In the words of Saint Augustine, "There are two types of charity: giving and forgiving. Giving all that you have received, forgiving all that you have suffered."[3]

Interestingly, this finds its confirmation in the very etymology of the word *forgive* in various languages. The English *forgive* (*for* + *give*), the French *pardonner* (*par*+*donner*), the German *vergeben* (*ver* + *geben*) all incorporate the core verb *to give*. Therefore, forgiving is giving for the sake of the other's dignity. In relation to God, it is seen as mercy, stemming not from pity or superiority, but from love and respect.

Without a doubt, God has a plan for us all, but one built on the foundations of care, patience, and willingness to give. This plan incorporates the time necessary for achieving maturity. God never forces us to do anything; He only sends us invitations!

All too often, we forget that He does not have to make excuses about His plans to us. He does not have

---

[3] **Augustine through the Ages: An Encyclopedia,** Published in 1999, by Eerdmans.

to explain why, but He surely does not ignore us either. Any attempts at explaining tragedy by anything that bears marks of negligence goes against the image of God, and the runaways only ensnare themselves in their unwillingness to forgive, driven by denial and negation. This can also lead to false forgiveness and attempts at a justification of tragedy. We try not to think about the pain and keep telling ourselves it would be a folly not to forgive such a triviality. It usually occurs when we are hurt by a person close to us. Real forgiveness requires us to deal with real emotions. Denial is a defensive mechanism that prevents us from tackling the problem at hand. However, this is not the point of true forgiveness that deals with true grudge. God, who truly cares about us, does not take remote control of our reality. He is not responsible for a DUI driver who runs over a group of passers-by. Still, He stands by those who suffer. He reminds them of still waters and green pastures. He tries to remind them that they are not some magical place to be discovered but a space within ourselves—a space within the heart transformed by God and filled with His presence.

The worst thing is not what happens to you but what you decide to do with it! Whatever is behind or ahead of you is of little importance compared to what is inside you!

Struggling with the reality that we cannot accept, we expect God to change it. At that point, we forget that God is indeed interested in change, but only that of the human heart. It does not mean He neither intervenes nor intervened in the reality (after all, we are aware of miraculous recoveries, the splitting of the Red Sea, the multiplication of the loaves, and many other examples), but in all this, he has always been most interested in the transformation of the human heart. Green pastures and still waters do not always mean a favorable turn of events in the reality around us. However, they always imply inner tranquility and peace within the human heart. This is what Jesus said when He pointed out that if somebody gets to know God, "Rivers of living water will flow from within them."[4]

It is sufficient to take a look at the lives of various biblical figures. Moses was called to lead his nation out of captivity. As it turned out, it was not only the captivity under their Egyptian overlords but also their own beliefs and attitudes. He was to carry out the mission while remaining the paragon of faith, obedience, and humility. The years during which he executed God's plan were full of struggle and hardship, and had it not been for the strength he received from God, he wouldn't have stood by his calling. He had the still waters and green pastures inside him!

David, even though he was called "a man after God's own heart," never had a peaceful life, but God worked in his heart. This is what gave birth to the words, "The Lord is my shepherd, I shall not want. He makes me lie down in green pastures; He leads me beside quiet waters"

---

[4] John 7:38

(Psalm 23:1–2).[5] Once he was made king of Israel, wars, conflicts, and conquests became his daily bread. It was no quiet or lazy life, but it still involved peacefulness and strength.

Jesus Himself never had it easy. However, it is very much unfounded to believe that He never remained in places full of God's peace and rest. The search of peace, quiet, strength, and hope in the world around us, our surroundings, education, work, social status, or even other people and their opinions does not make any sense! We will never find them in those places. The only thing we can do is deceive ourselves for a while.

When we are running away, we strongly wish for the reality around us to change. This is the only perspective that brings us a prospect of peace. There has to be a moment when we discover that it is all about us, not the ever-changing circumstances! God is all about me—as a person, not an aberrant vehicle of grievance!

Wounds multiply with time. Sometimes we try to console the sufferers by convincing them that there are worse forms of suffering. I would hear that on many occasions, and if it hadn't been for the shreds of decency I had in me and the belief that it was all said with good intentions, I would have punched many people in the face. So what if there are worse kinds of suffering! When we suffer, we always find a reason to show that our pain

---

[5] All Bible quotations hereinafter are taken from the New American Standard Bible (NASB) version.

is second to none. There is no scale to measure the level of suffering.

Accidents that claim many lives are usually considered more tragic than those in which only one person dies. However, this is not the perspective of those losing their loved ones. To a suffering heart, there is no difference!

It is worth remembering, as suffering is a common phenomenon. Research shows that even newborns express pain they undergo when they feel hungry. They don't understand what is going on, but they expect something to happen in order to ease their feeling of discomfort. Clinging to a breast, they discover that life consists of two separate stages: happiness, when they are full, and misery, when they are hungry. It makes no sense to persuade a small kid that others have had it worse. Stories about children starving in Africa will not bring them consolation.

A few years later, when their favorite toy breaks down, they will not be comforted by hearing that there are children who have never even seen such toys and would give everything to play even with a broken one.

Later, when they go through their first teenage heartbreak, they will not be cheered up by the fact that they are going to meet plenty of other interesting people.

Children suffer with all their hearts. Nothing much changes in the adult life.

A divorced wife suffers, uncomforted by the growing number of divorces. An unemployed father suffers, never consoled by the fact that other people around him also cannot find a job. A homeless family suffers, and they cannot be cheered up even if others around them lose all their possessions. Suffering is always overwhelming. Hearing that others suffer even more only increases the speed of the run. It does not matter whether we run due to an inability to forgive ourselves or another person, or perhaps as a result of events with no particular perpetrator. And so we run, screaming: Why? Comparing different cases of suffering only intensifies the feeling of being misunderstood. God has never discerned between those in need of help. Jesus saw equally to the blind, the crippled, prostitutes, and members of His time's clerical and military elites. It is not the mitigation of the loss, but it's concrete measurement that conditions forgiveness. Attempts at assuaging or downplaying the pain lead nowhere!

Now I know that the world is full of runaways. One of my favorite movies is *Forrest Gump* (1994), directed by Robert Zemeckis, based on a story by Winston Groom. It is a story about a mentally challenged and emotionally immature man, whose only way to deal with problems is by running away from them. Throughout the whole movie, a scream resounds: "Run, Forrest, run!"

The titular hero encounters many obstacles and odd situations in his life. Still, he carries on running.

In life, people run away because they have lost their

loved ones, their jobs, or anything else, but ultimately they all reach the point at which Forrest Gump said: "Life is like a box of chocolates. You never know what you're gonna get." This thought becomes the experience of runaways. They assume the stance of the movie hero and ... run. They believe it to be the only reasonable, and more importantly, the only possible solution. It becomes the means through which they express their protest against the injustice and its perpetrator. Filled with constantly growing pain, discomfort, and grief that become unbearable, they run.

In *The Problem of Pain,* C. S. Lewis thus describes the desire for escape:

> When I think of pain—of anxiety that gnaws like fire and loneliness that spreads out like a desert, and the heartbreaking routine of monotonous misery, or again of dull aches that blacken our whole landscape or sudden nauseating pains that knock a man's heart out at one blow ... If I knew any way of escape I would crawl through sewers to find it. [6]

Years passed, and I kept running. Work became my means of escape. I tried to work to the bone to silence the

---

[6] C. S. Lewis, The Problem of Pain, HarperColins Publisher 195 Broadway, New York, 2001, p. 105.

screaming heart. I filled my schedule to the very limits so as not to have the strength to think in the evenings. There were those who tried to convince me that it was only a matter of time, which supposedly heals all wounds. They explained that I would eventually find the strength to reconcile with God. This is another lie that can lead to false forgiveness. Time does not heal wounds. Time gives us distance, but it neither changes nor heals our hearts. Lack of forgiveness focuses on guilt, which is inerasable by time. The guilt of sin was not erased by the passing history, but through atonement and sacrifice. Something very real and concrete occurred in order to change the existing state of affairs!

The strength necessary for forgiveness isn't drawn from the passing of time. As days go by, they only show that one cannot run without a goal. When we are hurt, we expect compensation. We do not want to forget, even though forgetting is an important element of forgiving, accessible only to God.

When forgiving, the Almighty forgets all charges against us. However, He does not forget because somebody erased His memory. Even in heaven, there is no reset button next to the divine throne, pressed by a scrupulous angel every time God forgives. He does not remember our sins, which means that He does not take them into consideration. The Old Testament mentions the word *saloch*, literally meaning *forgiven debt*, forty-six times. Other words, also translatable as *to forgive—kapar* and *nasa*—infer that something has been atoned for, considered void. [7]By forgiving, God considers our guilt as irrelevant, repaid, atoned for, but not touched by amnesia. I will return to this thought later, when I tell the story of how I ultimately had to face the truth—about myself and about the wall of unforgiveness I had built around myself.

People Who Run ...

People who run share a few common traits. One of them is the conviction that nobody would ever be able to help them. They think they are on their own. From now on, they know best what their life should look like; so Lord, please let me and my children be! I am on the run!

Runaways live their lives deeply convinced that nobody understands them or knows what they feel when they are down. And even though their ages, roots, and education may vary, they all say the same thing: "God, I know better!"

"God, I know better what should happen to the people of Nineveh," said the prophet Jonah, the Bible's very own Forrest Gump, before he started his own run. He also tried to escape when God chose him as His emissary to the capital of Assyria. Its residents committed many sins. The prophet was given a mission: to warn them about the wrath of God and the impending punishment—destruction of

---

[7] Samuel Prideaux Tregelles (trans.), Gesenius, Hebrew and Chaldee Lexicon to the Old Testament Scriptures, p. 411.

the city. His task was to make them repent for all their atrocities and evil. This was the only way they could count for God's forgiveness.

This mission turned out to be hard for Jonah, because God wanted to save people who had hurt the Israelites. God was giving them a chance and Jonah, himself an Israelite, deemed otherwise. He believed that the people of Nineveh should receive a just punishment for all their wrongdoings. They were Israel's oppressors, and therefore they were to perish. They did not deserve forgiveness. The harmed nation deserved vengeance.

Nevertheless, God had a different plan, of which Jonah was well aware. During his conversation with God, he said, "Therefore [in order to forestall this I fled to Tarshish, for I knew that You are a gracious and compassionate God, slow to anger and abundant in lovingkindness, and one who relents concerning calamity" (Jonah 4:2). He was sure that he knew how the matters should have been dealt with, and therefore he set off on a rather unsafe journey. It is not without significance that when he refused to forgive, he chose to "flee to Tarshish from the presence of the LORD" (Jonah 1:3).

The prophet therefore decided to run and hide away from God. He boarded a ship that sailed in the direction opposite to Nineveh. Then, a tempest hit the sea, and the ship started to sink. Jonah knew that the sinister waves were a sign of the wrath of God that befell him because of his disobedience. In fact, when the horrified shipmates threw the escapee overboard, the storm calmed down.

Even though he had offended God, Jonah still received His help. This is yet another amazing feature of God, who does not deny the runaways His care and mercy. It was not only Jonah who could count on His help as he set out on a journey. When the people of Israel had to wander through a desert for forty years as a consequence of their sin, God still didn't deprive them of His care and mercy. At night, he led them with a pillar of fire. During the day, he led them with a pillar of smoke. God had mercy over Jonah and sent a giant fish to his rescue. In its stomach, the wretched runaway spent three days before he was thrown onto the shore. Thus, he experienced God's mercy and learned that even though he had failed Him, God forgave him his disobedience and again commanded him to go to Nineveh. Jonah went to the city and told its people of God for forty days. He struck faith in them and made them repent.

God forgave the people of Nineveh, but Jonah did not. He obediently carried out his mission but could not forgive all the harm that Israel had suffered.

When Jonah saw that God showed love to his brothers' oppressors, he left the city and decided to die, accusing God of being too gentle and merciful. He preferred death to forgiveness.

God then explained to Jonah patiently that one should always show compassion for other people, even if they were enemies—that one should be capable of mercy even if the culprit isn't asking for it or offering anything in return.

The "Lord, I know better" stance also became the sin of another biblical figure, Simon Peter, one of the twelve chosen by Jesus as His closest disciples.

The fisherman appointed to discipleship was considered the most important among them. He believed Jesus to be the Messiah, and it was him the Lord eventually trusted above all and despite everything by telling him to "tend his lambs" (John 21:15). Still, even he would on several occasions set off on a lonely run, distancing himself from God. It happened when Jesus first told His disciples about the torments awaiting him. Peter then said, "God forbid *it*, Lord! This shall never [happen to You'" (Matthew 16:22) Christ then replied, "Get behind Me, Satan!" (Matthew 16:23).

To tell the truth, this New Testament's Forrest did not run too far, but he still had his own idea and plan, and by running away from thinking by God's rules, he made mistakes. This is why he first tried to defend Jesus from capture with a sword in his hand, and he even cut off the ear of one of the assailants, just to reject Christ three times later on.

Peter was unable to accept that his Master had a different plan; he did not understand Christ's statement that the sense and aim of His coming to earth was to give His life on the cross. At that time, he also failed to comprehend that the harm done to His Son by evil people did not hinder God from forgiving.

It was only later that Peter understood the fact that Christ, even before he died and became resurrected, had forgiven His oppressors when they dealt Him the most painful blows by falsely accusing, hurting, and eventually crucifying Him.

According to a legend, Peter also attempted to flee from Rome when persecution of Christians commenced under Nero's orders. On his way he met Christ, who asked him, "Where are you going, Lord?" *Quo vadis, domine?* And so he turned back. He ceased to calculate according to human categories.

By building the wall of unforgiveness, runaways convince themselves that they are doing the right thing, because they have been treated unfairly. Having been hurt, we grow to believe that life treated us unjustly and we look forward to justice. On the run, we meet others, equally harrowed, disillusioned, hurt, looking for comfort in the escape. Running together, we mutually reinforce our erroneous thinking and get into even bigger trouble.

The inability to forgive leads to even greater embitterment and rejection and a growing sense of harm. We delve deeper and deeper into frustration and doubt, while forgiveness is not as much the consequence of faith as its prerequisite. In order to believe God and in God, one needs to accept forgiveness as the crux of Christian conduct. By not forgiving, we do not receive; by not receiving, we do not give. This is the way the lack of forgiveness ultimately destroys faith, not to be renewed unless unforgiveness is transformed into reconciliation.

Reconciliation requires mutuality, which is not necessarily the case with forgiveness. We know that Christ forgave His oppressors on the cross, even though we have no reason to believe that He had reconciled with any of them.

Harm implies a disturbance or complete destruction of a relationship, while forgiveness is an expression of willingness to fix it. However, commitment from both sides is necessary in order to rebuild the ties. Without forgiveness, reconciliation is impossible, but forgiving itself is an act that may take place regardless of the other side's reaction.

Living in unforgiveness, we push deeper into bitterness and anger, increasing our pain and suffering. What seems like protection from pain in fact becomes an endless torment that we inflict upon ourselves. When we run away and persist in unforgiveness, we are in for even bigger trouble.

Jonah, the Forrest Gump of the Old Testament, fell into raging sea waters. The thing that was supposed to bring stability and protection after several thousand miles turned out to be a pointless journey.

The New Testament's Forrest Gump, Peter, believed that bringing his own vision of defending both the Master and His gospel into life would bring him safety. Not only did he fail to achieve his goals, but he stooped even lower by betraying and denying Jesus and His teachings. Luckily, he turned away from that perilous path before long and mustered up the courage to preach about Christ under all circumstances, regardless of potential consequences.

What about the runaways of our times? Some plunge into chaos of mundaneness, some escape into work, relationships unworthy of their engagement, or a thick web of addictions. They all reach a lonely island, the only inhabitant of which is desolation.

The marathon of unforgiveness ends in the same way for everyone. We reach the finish line on the island of loneliness—exhausted, frustrated, embittered, and broken. Sometimes we desire vengeance for everything we have been put through—vengeance that leads to even more crimes and hurting! Not only does the lack of forgiveness consume us from the inside, but it can also become a motor of destructive actions against our surroundings and other people.

One of the bloodiest conflicts in twentieth-century Europe, the civil war in former Yugoslavia, was born out of unforgiveness that turned into a thirst for vengeance. The Serbs, driven by the memory of the lost Battle of Kosovo that put them under Turkish domination in 1389, were unable to forgive. Invaders and occupants changed. The distribution of power changed in the world, in Europe, even in the very Balkans, but the thirst for vengeance never changed. It pushed the combatants to ruthlessness. Fostered for generations, that grudge finally took thousands of lives.

For the runners, everything that brings even temporary relief is good. Like a bottomless pit, it is always there to let us sink even deeper.

My revenge was not to forgive. I wanted to show I would be all right on my own, without anybody's help. I made lots of mistakes at that time; all runaways get into trouble, after all. Jonah almost drowned and ended up inside a giant fish, while Peter turned from the most faithful disciple into a traitor.

All runaways reach a point that they find not to their liking. Everything around me was unsuitable: objectionable relationships, improper places, inappropriate coworkers, inadequate decisions. I caused pain to different people. It all led me to discover another truth about runaways. Even though we focus on ourselves when we run away from forgiveness, eventually we discover that our loved ones suffer along with us.

Harm leads people to believe that what they feel and think is of utmost importance. This turns the runaways into egocentrics who take all too long to notice that their family and friends also have to face the consequences of their escape.

When Jonah ran away onto the ship, his fellow sailors suffered with him. Not only did he find himself in danger, but he also jeopardized the people who had given him shelter. They wanted to help him and thus got into a serious predicament. Peter's escape also caused the One who had chosen, appointed, and loved him to suffer.

I ran and hid my tears away from my children; I tried not to show my pain. Little did I know that my run was tearing up their hearts even more, and I was not protecting them inasmuch as I was causing them to suffer. I did not realize that by loving me, they suffered doubly: because of what had taken place and because of watching someone they loved start a blind run.

My friends also suffered with me. It is yet another curious aspect of the marathon of unforgiveness. When suffering, we isolate ourselves, trying to protect our world, convinced we have every right to do so. We do not notice the tears and pain of those close to us. We suffer because we have been hurt, and by not forgiving, we hurt those we wish to protect.

Our loved ones ask, "What should we do? How can we influence this man? How can we ease his pain? How can we persuade him to forgive?"

Runaways do not listen to reason. They think they can run away from the truth. In reality, it is impossible.

I discovered I could run from God but never completely run away from God.

In all His wisdom, patience, humility, and love, He awaits the moment when the runaways discover how pointless their escape is. Running from God is running from the sense and aim of human existence. He does not compete with human emotions, disillusionment, sentiments, expectations, ideas, strivings, but he calmly and patiently stands at the door and knocks.

A moment comes when all runaways discover the truth that even though God and His offer can be ignored, it does not change the fact of His existence and the sacrifice He made for us not to run onto the lonely island but straight to our Father's gates. It is the moment when our belief that we have a reason not to forgive weakens and slowly ceases to be the driving force behind our actions.

And even though the runaways are resistant to influences and carry on their lonely run, at some point they are bound to face the truth and the One they were trying to run away from. They have to find out what He was doing while they were on the run.

Upon examination of the biblical runaways, we see that God did not abandon them, as He even stood by them in a very peculiar way. He stood by Jonah even when he was lacking humility. He remained with Peter in order to accept his apologies and invite him to His pastures. God never changed His intentions or plans. He unceasingly blessed David once he returned to Him. This is what runaways discover: we keep on running and running, while He remains unchangeably patient and repeats His offer.

By running, we do not change the reality around us. We change ourselves. We chase the wild goose by fighting the constantly haunting question: *Why?* What have we done to deserve this suffering? We change, and when the run of unforgiveness lasts for too long, the change is irreversible!

Where is justice? This is what the disadvantaged seek; this is what our unforgiveness demands! We are unable to forgive as long as we feel unfairly treated. However, we never ask ourselves what justice is. We think that *justice* means that somebody is punished, but that sounds more like revenge.

The classic definition of justice was coined by the Roman lawyer Ulpian, according to whom justice is the constant and perpetual will to render to every man his due (*Iustitia est constans et perpetua voluntas ius suum cuique tribuere*). It infers that when we are hurt, we feel entitled to demand others to get what they deserve. Justice must be served. In spite of the fact that we know that *justly* does not mean *the same* or *equally to everybody*, we still struggle to think of any kind of justice other than that which fully compensates for our suffering. It seems, however, that justice is done when everything is in its right place, right there where it's supposed to be. This is what God's justice basically is about. He has the same kind of forgiveness and redemption for everybody, while He does not treat everybody the same. In His justice, He does not expect to find us in a context different from what He has planned for us. Running away from the truth, evading reality, we are not in the place we are supposed to be! Lack of forgiveness is an injustice that we inflict, driven by our pain and sense of harm. The lawful God has prepared a place for everybody in the undisturbed, eternal harmony of His presence. His will is for everybody, according to the rights He has bestowed upon us, to end up in the place of their destiny—the eternity. Nevertheless, humankind chose injustice; we left, ran away, rebelled, and distanced ourselves from the place of our destiny and then the righteous God, in all His mercy and love, followed us through Jesus, so that justice triumphs and everybody is where they are supposed to be.

Unfortunately, the runaways refuse to live by the rights ascribed to them! God did not plan a punishing marathon but goodness and peace for all humankind. The escape is therefore an injustice brought upon themselves by the runaways, and stopping them is the only right step toward justice. By demanding justice, I demanded something that I did not practice toward myself.

I demanded punishment and justice while expecting and enjoying mercy for myself. Even the runaways realize that they are beneficiaries, they have neither earned nor deserved what they get. We have received proof of merciful treatment. I also discovered that what I had received was a consequence of mercy, capable of restoring justice. It hit me with full force: I could not run anymore as I wouldn't find much in the escape.

Jesus's parable of the shepherd leaving ninety-nine of his sheep to find the missing one is no fair treatment of the whole flock but an expression of mercy that restores justice to the lost one. Mercy that is understood not exclusively as a display of undeserved favor. If it only came out of the need for kindness, it wouldn't have enough impact to lift what has fallen and rebuild what has been demolished. It would be merely a phenomenon recurring according to the present need!

Mercy given to us by God is His attitude. I cannot deserve it, earn it, fight for it, or invent it. *There is absolutely nothing I can do to be loved more, but there is also absolutely nothing I can do, by running away, hiding, or holding grudges, to be loved less.*

The biblical story about vineyard workers working at different times of the day, yet still receiving the same remuneration, does not show the kind of justice we usually expect. It's a story of a good and merciful God who patiently accepts everybody, offering the same forgiveness and redemption. Even though *fairly* does not mean *equally*, the gracious God sees to it that we all find ourselves in our places in a fair manner.

The discovery of the fact that the justice we demand is not about revenge and compensation as much as it is about taking our place changes the dynamics of the run. If I am not running for justice, then what am I running for? What is my goal? What is my destiny? And despite the pleasing fact that God has planned eternity for everybody, even though not everybody is willing to accept it, the basic question remains of our place here on earth, where we feel hurt and mauled. There are two most important moments in all people's lives: when they are born, and when they discover why.

Personally, I eventually understood that He had not changed His calling for me. I was to keep being the person I had been so far! He had not rearranged anything; I had to face the consequences of my escape. I had to apologize to those I had hurt and repair what I had destroyed. At that time, I already knew that I was to begin a new journey, but this time not blindly. The journey was called forgiveness. And even though I had already stopped crying for God to leave me and my children alone, I still couldn't muster up for that vital gesture. It is not enough to discover that somebody loves us. It is not enough to discover that He only wishes well for us. It is not enough to stop and say, "*I forgive.*"

Forgiveness does not come in a hurry. It also doesn't come with time; as I have already mentioned, it is not in the passing of time that the power of forgiveness lies. I felt like my eleven-year-old son, who cried, "I'm worried I will forget what mom looked like!" The runaways discover that they ran because they were scared. They were scared of life, memories, or what was still to happen. Not forgiving is easier than finding the strength to act. Fear is much more powerful a motivation than peace, hatred is more powerful than reconciliation, and unforgiveness is more powerful than forgiveness.

A moment had to come for me to do something about it, but I still wasn't ready to forgive God. However, not only Him. There was the culprit I already knew had driven the car of that type for the first time, not to mention it was overloaded, which impacted its maneuverability on turns. There were also people who suspected that my life must have been full of sin, since so much misery happened to me. There were also those who tried to convince my children that the accident was my fault.

How much would I like to forget how painful lies, deceit, betrayal, and death are. I knew that blissful obliviousness did not exist—that for some reason human memory stored pain and hurt. I knew it, and I know it to this day, that memory can switch itself off, but it only happens in a mechanical manner as the body's defense against something that could destroy it. Silencing the memories also doesn't bring the desired peace.

Unfortunately, some things cannot be forgotten. However, it is not time and forgetfulness that are important in the process of forgiveness, but what we do with what we remember. I am glad that God forgets my sins, but I have to deal with my memory on my own. I cannot count on time to do something with it. Step by step, I discovered that in order to forgive, I had to define and accurately name the reason of my suffering; I had to call my pain by its name. I had to shed myself of everything I covered it with and reveal the long-hidden reality.

Forgiveness is not something we exhibit, yet it is something that we show.

In order to draw such a conclusion, I had to take yet

another journey. However, this time it wasn't a lonely run, but a trip in the company of those who had stood by me. Something like this always happens at the beginning of every healing. Refusing to run does not mean stopping but starting a new journey, which is by no means easier, but definitely better.

Chapter 3

Life and Shadow in Neverland

We try to follow the new path, but we are unsure as to what to do with the burden we carry inside. What shall we do with the reality we carry within ourselves? Similarly to the previous one, this journey does not offer a reset button. Our knowledge, convictions, and emotions still refuse to go together. We know what's about to happen, but we still don't know why.

I knew I could not silence my feelings. I discovered that the help offered to me would not bring me relief. I had to find the way to freedom, the way to rid myself from the burden I was carrying.

But how was I supposed to do it? By trying to understand? No, I was unable to comprehend or accept it! Despite the years of effort and marathon running, I had changed nothing.

So where was the beginning of the path I was supposed to take? Where was the path to the liberation and transformation of the embittered, tormented, and hopeless heart into a beating, hopeful heart, filled with love of life and freedom?

One of my favorite childhood books was a story by the Scottish writer James Matthew Barrie. Based on an earlier theatrical play, it was titled *The Adventures of Peter Pan*. The main protagonist was a playful boy who never wanted to grow up. He led a life full of adventures in a realm called Neverland. His best friend was a fairy by the name of Tinkerbell. Naturally, there was also the deadly villain—Capitan Hook.

At that time, I wasn't aware that the hero's name was not coincidental. The real Peter lost his mom to cancer at a young age. However, the inspiration for the titular hero came from the author's brother David, who died in an ice-skating accident at the age of thirteen.

Barrie wrote the book for his mother, who never recovered from the death of one of her sons.

It's fascinating that the book I zealously read in my youth had been born out of pain, struggle with suffering, and attempts to escape. Unfortunately, it described something more than a mere fairytale. Even though Neverland is a beautiful island where everything can be perfect, its biggest problem is that it doesn't exist!

Trying to find the way to freedom, I found myself in the Neverland I had created for myself. I created a hermetically closed world, where nothing was real but pain and bitterness. I had different people around me, but I was connected with them through kind acquaintance rather than true, deep friendship.

We very often escape to Neverland, building an unreal world around ourselves. Reality on this nonexistent island is deprived of truth. Many ideas in our lives are just empty slogans; we speak of tolerance, but it's hard to encounter it in real life. We speak of mutual respect, but we deem it inappropriate to think against the general opinion. We demand acceptance, but it is better not to stand out too much. We create quasi-societies, we build quasi-relationships that lack the most important things. Unfortunately, it is sometimes the case in the church as well; after all, it possesses clearly laid down rules of faith, values, and norms, which very few remember in real life. Forgiveness is one of the most fundamental rules of the church, yet we rarely forgive. We preach unity, yet divisions in the church come all too easily.

Searching for the strength to forgive, we have to accept that the only way leading to it is the truth. "And you will know the truth, and the truth will make you free" (John 8:32). We need to accept what we really feel, the who and the where of ourselves; what lies ahead of us and for us; and where our real and rightful place is. Once we truly face our thoughts, claims, and feelings, only then can we move on. Therefore, we have to muster up the courage to face ourselves. If we wish to forgive somebody else, we have to see if we can forgive ourselves in the first place. In order to offer forgiveness to somebody, not only do I need to know my state but also the truth about myself. God accepts me just the way I am, not to make me stay the same but to make me develop and improve.

Jesus clearly stated that one of the two most important things to man is the principle of love: "You shall love your neighbor as yourself" (Matthew 22:39).

We live in an unfair world, as we have not been in the right place ever since, "All have turned aside, together they have become useless; There is none who does good, There is not even one" (Romans 3:12). Our Maker wants to see us in complete harmony with Him. "For God so loved the world, that He gave His only begotten Son, that whoever believes in Him shall not perish, but have eternal life" (John 3:16).

Deep in the darkness of suffering and unforgiveness, we learn to be the way people want to see us. We hide behind the screen of obligation. Neverland, here we come! Everywhere we go, we keep hearing what we are supposed to be like. In *The Life You've Always Wanted*, John Ortberg writes:

> The great danger that arises when we don't experience authentic transformation is that we will settle for what might be called pseudo-transformation. We know that as Christians we are called to "come out and

be separate," that our faith and spiritual commitment should make us different somehow. But if we are not marked by greater and greater amounts of love and joy, we will inevitably look for substitute ways of distinguishing ourselves from those who are not Christians.[8]

Trapped in the web of expectations, we create a system of behavior and characteristics of a believer. If we do not experience the things we hear about in the church, we hide our lack of faith, honesty, devotion, trust, and love behind specific behaviors that are supposed to indicate the deep spirituality of the practitioner.

In a lecture during a church leadership conference, Brene Brown said, "The rougher week we've had, the better we look in the church."

This way, we create something that the Bible calls hypocrisy, and which in psychological terms was dubbed by C. G. Jung as "shadow."

To put it simply, the shadow is the part of our psyche that has become the hiding place for all the features, attitudes, or modes of behavior that we know are undesirable. When we don't forgive, we know that we are expected to do the reverse thing, so we hide our wounds deep inside the shadow so that nobody else sees them.

---

[8] John Ortberg, *The Life you always wanted*, Published September 29th 2002 by Zondervan, page 23

However, our shadow is prone to manifest itself in the way we view other people and the reality around us. We project our shadow onto others. Our perception of the world is distorted as we notice in others what has become our shadow, what's hidden deep inside ourselves.

It is hard to accept at first, but the truth is that very often we ascribe to other people the things we do not wish to recognize about ourselves. This is why everybody else irritates and unnerves us so much.

In order to forgive and break free, we have to truly commit ourselves to God—completely, not only in the religious aspect.

How does one recognize one's shadow? As always, there is an abundance of ways. One of them is through conscious observation of what irritates us in other people. Perhaps you are annoyed by somebody's arrogance because you can never have it your way? Perhaps you get mad when somebody makes a mess because as a perfectionist you never indulge in messiness, although you do have a tad of a slob in you? And perchance, if you are bugged by somebody's laziness, it is only because you can't take it easy, even though a part of you would like to be lazy from time to time?

I myself am horribly annoyed by irresponsible people. I usually take responsibility for everything, even if I shouldn't, and sometimes it does not end well for me. On the way to real forgiveness, there is no place for pretending. That was one of my most important discoveries. Never again will I pretend that my problem had nothing to do with God.

I couldn't deal with the things for which I still blamed him. And I think I am not a particularly unique case. From our youngest years, we are taught that there is no place for such thoughts and feelings. But what should we do when we are hit by the nagging question: *Why?*

We ask this question in an act of helplessness; we try to thwart our feelings. We shout it out when nobody can hear us. But the problem is: even if we don't speak, He still hears and knows!

The truth is, we very often blame God for everything. So did I, carrying my wounds and sense of hurt. When we forgive, we must not replace the real world with a candy land. Hiding in the shadow and living in the unreality of Neverland blocks us from noticing what is real.

Unforgiveness entraps us in a strange land, with real people nowhere to be found, not to mention the real God, as such does not exist in quasi-relationships.

He will not find a place for Himself in a quasi-healed heart, quasi-expressed love. He truly sacrificed His Son for us. Christ truly suffered, truly loves, and there is nothing He can do if I am not ready for the truth. Suffering is always very real and true. The anger of unforgiveness is also very real. The sense of rejection also truly hurts, so no half-measures will be able to remedy it.

Yes, now I understand: it was my journey to Neverland and back.

Chapter 4

Forgiveness 101

Stopping my escapist run would not bring me any relief. Discovering that there had to be some way to freedom would not free me from the emotions that were tearing me apart. I knew that forgiveness could not be based on repressing what I felt. It was neither denial nor forgetfulness, because I still remember. There is no pretending that nothing happened. Whatever hurts or harms us is real and very often irreversible.

I tried to rebuild my life, even though I knew that nothing would reverse the effects of what happened on December 5, 2003. I still knew that in order to free myself from the trap of sorrow, bitterness, and frustration, I had to discover what forgiveness was.

Do you remember the parable from the gospel of Matthew 18:21–35? The king had erased the debt of one of his servants. Nevertheless, the servant was unable to do the same thing for his debtor, despite the fact that the debt was considerably smaller. Having seen this, the king revoked his decision and punished the ungrateful servant.

This gospel story begins with the question that Peter asked Jesus: "Then Peter came and said to Him, 'Lord, how often shall my brother sin against me and I forgive him? Up to seven times?' Jesus said to him, 'I do not say to you, up to seven times, but up to seventy times seven'" (Matthew 18:21–22).

In Jewish culture, the number seven represents wholeness. The term *seventy seven times* can imply infinity. What comes out of this use of symbols? There still isn't any answer as to what forgiveness is and how it works.

It isn't hard to imagine that Peter knew that according to rabbinical teachings, man was to forgive his brother three times. Rabbi Jose ben Hanina once said, "He who begs forgiveness from his neighbor must not do so more than three times. ... If a man commits an offence once, they forgive him; if he commits an offence a second time they forgive him; if he commits an offence a third time they forgive him; the fourth time they do not forgive."[9]

Peter's offer therefore sounded like a spiritual bargain, along the lines of God's resolution after Cain killed his brother, whereby he clearly warned, "Whoever kills Cain, vengeance will be taken on him sevenfold" (Genesis 4:15).

---

[9] William Barclay, The Gospel of Matthew, Volume 2, Westminster John Knox Press, Louisville, Kentucky 2001, p. 225.

TO FORGIVE GOD!

Jesus surprises! Not for the first time, of course. With His response, He alludes to the Old Testament story, making it clear that He has read Peter's intentions. It was a strategy typical of Jesus, who didn't always respond directly to the question. Even though the question was specific, Jesus answered with a parable.

From the mouth of Lamech, the Bible's first bigamist called by his name, come the words: "If Cain is avenged sevenfold, Then Lamech seventy and sevenfold" (Genesis 4:24).

When Peter asks about sevenfold forgiveness, referring to Cain's story, Jesus alludes to Cain's descendants. Avenged? Peter and Jesus speak about the right to revenge. Something bad happened to you: you were harmed, hurt, deceived—you have the right to demand something in return, you have the right to retaliate. Is this not what a broken heart calls for? May something happen. May something compensate for my pain!

Is this not the loudest sound of unforgiveness?

From Peter and Jesus's conversation comes something else: *forgiveness is a type of attitude that gives up on the right to retaliate.*

It by no means implies that we don't have a right to it. In the parable told by Jesus, the servant released from debt still had the right to demand his debtor to pay back his due. But this is not why the king punished him! The punishment was administered for the lack of love and understanding toward the second debtor.

Forgiveness is the moment when the truth reaches me—that in spite of what I feel, in spite of what I am struggling with, I forgot my right to take revenge or retaliate for whatever happened to me. I stop expecting compensation.

I finally realized that God was not ignoring my feelings. He was mindful of my suffering but at the same showed that if He does not require revenge, I should do the same.

It is fascinating that in all His generosity, all His lavishly offered grace, God treated forgiveness in a different manner. When it comes to love, God is limitlessly generous. When we search for peace, He gives it to us with no prescription. When we miss Him, nothing will stop Him. When we look for understanding, He is limited by nothing.

However, when it comes to forgiveness, God has set a clear rule. It is strange, but it is in forgiving, meaning giving up the right to revenge, that God has set the boundaries. He clearly stated, "I will not demand vengeance if you do the same." "Just as the Lord forgave you, so also should you" (Colossians 3:13). Suffice it to mention one more well-known sentence in which we ask for equal treatment: "And forgive us our debts, as we also have forgiven our debtors" (Matthew 6:12).

Jesus Himself is the most accurate on the subject of forgiveness: "For if you forgive others for their transgressions, your heavenly Father will also forgive

TO FORGIVE GOD!

you. But if you do not forgive others, then your Father will not forgive your transgressions" (Matthew 6:14–15).

God put the fate of forgiveness in our hands. He is ready to grant it with no limits, but He also gives us a responsibility. Jesus speaks of it, and Jacob and Paul write about it. And thus the forgiveness that I am looking for in God depends on what I do with the one in my hands.

Why is that so? It is the way the Father shows respect to His Son, who "emptied himself,"[10] although He didn't have to, as He was without fault. Jesus decided to give up on that which he was entitled to, in spite of what He felt. And it might sound like blasphemy, but when I read about the way Jesus prayed when He expressed His dependency on His Father, how He asked for the cup to pass away from Him,[11] how He cried about loneliness on the cross—I know that what He did, He did in spite of what He felt in his heart. Fully divine, and yet completely human, He felt the same things as you and me. His heart, even though it was not filled with unforgiveness, knew of rejection, disrespect, harm, betrayal, and pain. He knew, but He didn't demand vengeance; He chose the cross.

God the Father does not allow even a single drop of Christ's blood to go to waste. He does not allow the sacrifice of His Son to be deprived of dignity and recognition. I believe this to be the reason why He established this single rule:

---
[10] See Philippians 2:7.
[11] See Matthew 26:39.

> I will grant you forgiveness of all kinds, without any payment or compensation for what you have done. Your debt will be erased completely, but please remember—it does not happen just like that. My Son paid the highest price for it. Therefore, I do not wish you to accept His sacrifice and then do nothing with it! I know your heart! I know you, and I love you very much! I cry with you and I suffer with you, but if you want freedom, please accept the one I have for you, and don't keep it just for yourself. Give up on your right to revenge, just the way I have!

This is more or less the conversation I had with God. I felt truly loved, accepted, understood, and embraced. I found out that He had never forgotten me and knew exactly what I had been going through and already carried it on His shoulders.

What I spoke about with God has to be heard and discovered by each and every runaway. This way, they will never succumb to the treacherous advice: "Run, Forrest, run!" and cease to run away, just like Jonah and Peter did. They will understand that forgiveness is not a matter of time but of treading down the path of truth and giving up the right to retaliation.

If even the biblical heroes who witnessed God's grace

could not at once find the strength for forgiveness, it surely doesn't come easy.

But if God so consistently and patiently encourages us to do it, it must be good. And surely, it is God who can open up our hearts and give us the strength to forgive.

Epilogue

Where did I find myself on my new way? I stopped, and this is what I had to say:

Father, you know how much it hurts. You know how hurt, abandoned, and mistreated I feel.

Only you know how much I would like to understand and know why.

Father, I now understand that you really know. You know me, and you know everything about me. You don't ignore me and my feelings. You patiently listen to my screams and claims. With love, You observe my struggle and try to convince me that nothing happened!

I testify that I still do not understand and I still do not know, but I lay it all down before You. I give it all up, because for me, You gave up on the right to compensation!

One more thing, Father—I love You and I ask of You: please provide for me and my children!

About the Author

Father of two children, former University Teacher, pastor of a local church involved in Leadership Development wrote about his journey of forgiveness after tragic death of his wife. He is writing about Christian faith when thing are not going well.

Made in the USA
Lexington, KY
31 May 2016